HISTORY'S
FORGOTTEN EVENTS

by Rachel A. Bailey

www.12StoryLibrary.com

12-Story Library is an imprint of Bookstaves.

Photographs ©: Popperfoto/Getty Images, cover, 1; The Boston Daily Globe/PD, 4; PD, 4; BPL/PD, 5; PD, 6; PD, 7; Brian Whitmarsh/CC2.0, 8; PD, 8; Daderot/PD, 9; BiblioArchives/LibraryArchives/CC2.0, 10; kai keisuke/Shutterstock.com, 11; PD, 12; PD, 13; Kokoo/CC2.5, 14; PD, 15; Library of Congress, 15; Norfolk Southern Corporation, 16; PD, 17; Vintage Images/Getty Images, 18; PD, 19; The Mariner's Chronicle/PD, 20; Library of Congress, 21; PD, 21; Bain News Service/PD, 22; Ellen/CC2.0, 23; alan farrow/PD, 24; Trinity Mirror/Mirrorpix/Alamy Stock Photo, 25; Portland Evening Telegram/PD, 26; PD, 27; WitR/Shutterstock.com, 28; overcrew/Shutterstock.com, 29

ISBN
978-1-63235-596-6 (hardcover)
978-1-63235-650-5 (paperback)
978-1-63235-709-0 (ebook)

Library of Congress Control Number: 2018938111

Printed in the United States of America
Mankato, MN
July 2018

About the Cover

The last boats evacuating from Saint-Pierre in Martinique. The volcanic cloud from Mount Pelée is in the background.

Access free, up-to-date content on this topic plus a full digital version of this book. Scan the QR code on page 31 or use your school's login at 12StoryLibrary.com.

Table of Contents

Molasses Floods Boston's North End

It was a mild winter day on the waterfront. On January 15, 1919, people in Boston's North End went about their day. City workers ate their lunch. Firemen played cards. Children walked home from school.

A view of the molasses tank before it burst.

Nearby, molasses leaked from a large tank. United States Industrial Alcohol (USIA) owned the tank. The US government needed the molasses to create munitions during World War I. The war had ended two months earlier.

Around 12:30 p.m., witnesses heard a dull roar and rumble. It sounded like something was shaking. Within seconds, the tank lid burst. The circular walls snapped into two giant pieces. Molasses plowed through the city. The sticky mass traveled at 35 miles per hour (56 km/h). It destroyed city blocks, toppled buildings, and damaged vehicles. The molasses reached up to 40 feet high (12 m).

Twenty-one people were killed in the Great Molasses Flood. People and animals drowned trying to escape the hardening syrup. Workers were crushed by buildings that fell on

The destruction after the flood.

top of them. Rescuers found some firemen at their card game. They were buried in the wreckage.

After the tragedy, several lawsuits were filed against USIA. It was found that the tank walls were too thin to support the molasses. Finally, in 1925, the company agreed to pay family members and flood victims $628,000. That's about $8 million in today's dollars.

2.3 million
Gallons of molasses (8.7 million L) that flooded Boston's North End.

- The molasses burst out of a large tank.
- Many lives were lost.
- Years later, the molasses company paid heavy fines.

THINK ABOUT IT

Many people drowned in the molasses. Was it right to hold USIA responsible? Do you think the company paid enough in fines?

Deadly Volcano Buries City in Minutes

Saint-Pierre is a town in Martinique, an island in the Caribbean Sea. Overlooking the town is Mount Pelée, a 4,500-foot volcano. In April 1902, witnesses noticed steam coming out of the mountain. Many complained that the steam had a foul odor. Weeks later, the earth rumbled and the mountain shot black smoke into the air. The smoke turned into ash that was white as snow.

People worried about the mountain's strange activities. Scientists studied the volcano. They concluded that it was safe. Politicians told residents to focus on the local elections. These were just weeks away.

Early on the morning of May 8, ants and centipedes sensed something terrible was about to happen. They scurried down the mountain, attacking people in their path. Next came the snakes. They slithered to the land below.

At 8 a.m., Mount Pelée erupted. A wave of boiling mud and fire slammed into Saint-Pierre. Within minutes, 30,000 people died. Trees fell on their sides. Houses toppled over. Only two residents survived Mount Pelée's fury.

The eruption in 1902.

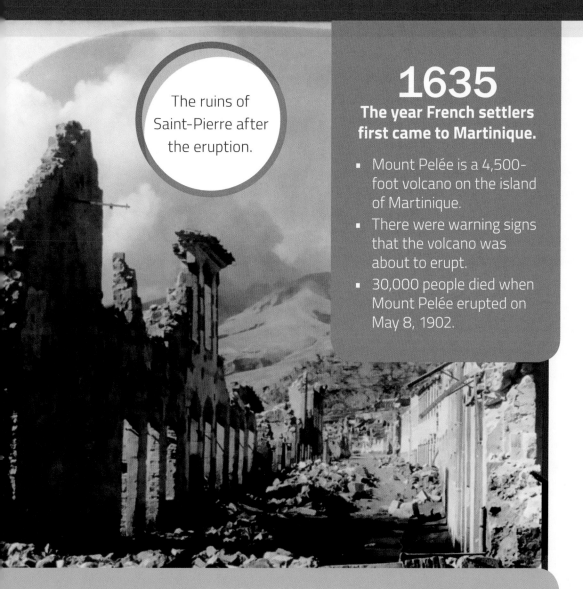

The ruins of Saint-Pierre after the eruption.

1635
The year French settlers first came to Martinique.

- Mount Pelée is a 4,500-foot volcano on the island of Martinique.
- There were warning signs that the volcano was about to erupt.
- 30,000 people died when Mount Pelée erupted on May 8, 1902.

PRISONER SURVIVES

When Mount Pelée erupted, a man named Ludger Sylbaris was in a prison cell. Light and air came in through a narrow slit in the door. Suddenly, light changed to darkness. Sylbaris heard crashing, roaring, thudding, and grinding sounds. The air got very hot, making it difficult to breath. Superheated mud and sand flowed in through the slit. Sylbaris's lower body was burned. Then everything went silent. Days later, rescuers found him. He was badly injured, but alive.

Steamboat Found in Kansas Cornfield

The steamboat *Arabia* was built in Pennsylvania in 1853. In 1855, it began traveling to towns along the Missouri River. On August 30, 1856, the *Arabia* left St. Louis for the last time. Seven days later, it docked in Kansas City. That evening, workers unloaded some freight.

The *Arabia* then continued up the river while many passengers ate dinner. Suddenly the boat slammed into a walnut tree under the water. The tree pierced the *Arabia's* hull. The boat leaned to the left. Water covered the main deck. Cargo slid across the floor. Passengers scrambled to get off the deck.

One lifeboat ferried passengers to the riverbank while the boat sank in 15 feet of water. All 130 passengers survived. In the rush, a mule was left

Illustration of the steamboat *Arabia.*

8

Contents unearthed from the *Arabia*.

behind and drowned. He had been tied to equipment on the boat's deck.

Over the next several years, the Missouri River shifted a half-mile. In 1987, a man named David Hawley and his family found the *Arabia* 45 feet under a farmer's cornfield. Today the boat and its contents are housed in a museum in Kansas City.

MOVING WEST

During the 1800s, scores of Americans and immigrants headed west. They wanted to start new lives. Some people walked, rode horses, or traveled in wagons. Some went by steamboat. A steamboat could move upstream and carry passengers' personal belongings. Many people started towns near the Missouri River. Steamboats also carried merchandise for these developing towns.

400
Number of steamboats that sank in the Missouri River.

- The steamboat *Arabia* sank after three years of service.
- The *Arabia* sank after it hit an underwater tree trunk.
- All 130 passengers survived.

Canadian Kids Boycott Candy Bars

April 23, 1947, was a sad day for a group of boys in British Columbia, Canada. After lunch, they visited the Wigwam Café in Ladysmith, a town on Vancouver Island. One brought a nickel to buy a candy bar. Instead, he had a rude surprise. The price of a candy bar had risen from five cents to eight cents.

Seventeen-year-old Parker Williams decided to do something about the jump in price. He helped organize a boycott. He drove his car up and down the street. Many kids crammed into the vehicle with him. Others followed behind with picket signs. One sign said, "Don't Buy 8¢ Bars. Lower Prices To 5¢. We Are Smart!"

News of the strike spread. Soon children in other Canadian cities and provinces began protesting. In Victoria, children stormed into government buildings. They raced

MOVING WEST

During World War II, the Canadian government subsidized chocolate. After the war, it stopped doing that. In 1947, a disease was attacking West Africa's cocoa bean plants. Chocolate is made from cocoa beans. Because of the disease, the beans were in short supply. Manufacturers had to pay more for them. So they charged buyers more.

3,000
Number of teens in Toronto who pledged to stop buying candy bars.

- In 1947, children from many parts of Canada boycotted candy bars.
- Candy bar prices had increased by three cents.
- The boycott stopped after newspapers reported that the protests were run by Communists.

through the halls chanting, "We want five-cent candy bars!"

Candy bar sales at one movie theater fell from 200 per night to 40 per night. A Vancouver store owner finally gave into the pressure. He dropped the price of candy bars back down to five cents.

Newspapers started reporting that the protests were being run by Communists. The protests stopped soon after.

5

Many New Yorkers Move on Same Day

Imagine moving into a new home while almost everyone around you is doing the same thing. That's what every May 1 was like in New York City for hundreds of years. It started in the seventeenth century, when the city was founded.

This is how it worked. On February 1, landlords notified tenants of rent increases. Renters had until May 1 to move if they did not like the new price. They paid workers called cartmen to move their goods. The cartmen used horses and large carts to transport items. They often charged people up to a week's wages before they would agree to help them. This was illegal, but many cartmen got away with it.

Moving Day was chaotic. Many schools closed. Horses and carts clogged the streets. Movers smashed

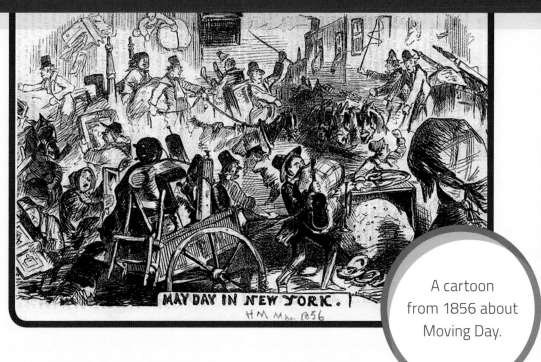

MAY DAY IN NEW YORK.
HM Mar 1856

A cartoon from 1856 about Moving Day.

mirrors and banged up furniture in their haste. People brought drapes and carpet from their old homes only to find that they would not fit in the new ones.

This practice went on until the end of the nineteenth century. Then October 1 became the new Moving Day. Many people left their city homes in May and lived in country houses for the summer. They didn't want to pay double rent. They put their items in storage until they came back to the city.

Moving Day died out after World War II. War veterans couldn't find homes when they returned to the city. People were staying put. There were not enough homes for everyone.

1 million

Estimated number of New Yorkers who moved on May 1 when Moving Day was at its height.

- Moving Day started in the seventeenth century.
- New Yorkers had until May 1 to move before their rents went up.
- Moving Day ended after World War II because of the housing shortage.

13

Orphans Carry Vaccine to Stop Smallpox

Starting in the 1500s, Spanish explorers came to the Americas. They didn't know it, but they brought smallpox with them. Millions of Aztec and Incan people died.

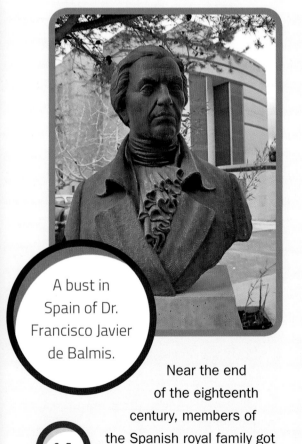

A bust in Spain of Dr. Francisco Javier de Balmis.

Near the end of the eighteenth century, members of the Spanish royal family got sick with smallpox. The brother of King Charles IV became infected and died. By then, the smallpox vaccine had been created.

The King learned that Spanish colonists in South America were dying from smallpox. In 1803, he paid for an expedition to bring the vaccine to them. The expedition was led by Dr. Francisco Javier de Balmis. There was no refrigeration to keep the vaccine alive on the long journey. So the vaccine was carried inside the bodies of 22 orphans.

Before the expedition left Spain, nurses gave two orphans the smallpox vaccine. Cysts formed on the orphans' arms. The cysts had pus in them. Before the pus dried up, some was put on the arms of two more orphans. This continued until the boat reached land. The orphans made a human chain of vaccine carriers.

3 out of 10

Number of people who used to die after catching smallpox.

- Smallpox wiped out millions of Aztecs and Incans.
- In 1803, Dr. Francisco Javier de Balmis led an expedition to stop smallpox in the Americas.
- Smallpox has now been wiped out all over the world.

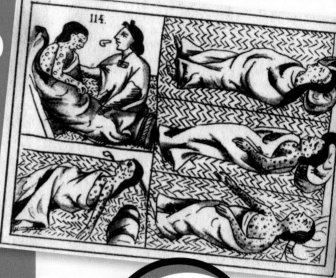

16th-century drawing of Aztec smallpox victims.

The last known case of smallpox was in 1977. A terrible disease has been wiped out.

COWS SAVE THE DAY

The smallpox vaccine was invented by Edward Jenner, an English doctor. When Jenner was a boy, he noticed that milkmaids sometimes got sores on their hands. Then they came down with a harmless disease called cowpox. After that, they never caught smallpox. Years later, in 1796, Jenner gave a young boy cowpox, then exposed him to smallpox. The boy didn't get smallpox. A vaccine was on the way.

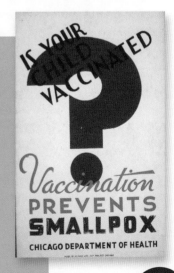

IS YOUR CHILD VACCINATED?

Vaccination PREVENTS SMALLPOX

CHICAGO DEPARTMENT OF HEALTH

7

Heavy Rains Cause Tragic Train Wreck

On July 1, 1889, the Norfolk and Western Passenger Train No. 2 arrived in Roanoke, Virginia. The train left the station just before midnight. On board were 56 passengers and 18 crew members.

It had been raining hard for the past 24 hours. Railroad crews worked to clear water from the tracks. As the train slowly moved toward the small town of Thaxton, rain pelted the area. It was hard for the conductor to see in the dark and the storm. He didn't know that Wolf Creek had flooded. The small creek had become a wide, rushing river.

16

2015

Year when a historical marker was placed near the site of the wreck.

- The wreck happened in Thaxton, Virginia, on July 2, 1889.
- Heavy rains had turned a small creek into a river.
- At least 18 people died.
- The wreck is one of the worst in the history of Virginia.

The water was eight to ten feet deep in some places. It had washed out part of a hill the track ran on. The track was now suspended over a chasm.

At 1:25 a.m., Train No. 2 inched forward. The earth collapsed under its weight. The train plunged into the creek below. The boiler exploded. Debris scattered all over the train. The train's gas lamps caught the debris on fire. Passengers were trapped inside the burning cars.

THINK ABOUT IT

The Thaxton train wreck happened in 1889. The historical marker went up 126 years later. Why is it important to remember events that took place long ago?

K 160
1889 THAXTON TRAIN WRECK

On 2 July 1889, a heavy storm turned nearby Wolf Creek into a raging river. The railroad embankment known as Newman's Fill, just north of here, became saturated. About 1:25 AM, it collapsed under the weight of Norfolk & Western Passenger Train Number Two, heading east from Roanoke. The train plunged into the washout. Survivors remained stranded for hours, while passengers trapped inside died in a fire that ripped through the wreckage. At least 18 people perished in one of Virginia's worst railroad accidents. In Cleveland, Tennessee, a monument was erected to honor three young residents killed in the wreck.

DEPARTMENT OF HISTORIC RESOURCES, 2014

Many could not escape. At least 18 people died and 21 were injured.

The weather was bad and communication was hard. It took five hours for helpers to arrive. The Thaxton train wreck was one of the deadliest in Virginia's history.

17

Mail Carriers Deliver Children through the Mail

Parcel post service began on January 1, 1913. Before then, Americans could only send packages through the mail that weighed four pounds or less. Now they could send packages weighing up to 11 pounds. In the first six months, millions of packages were mailed. Food, medicine, clothing, and other items could be delivered right to people's homes.

Soon after parcel post started, an Ohio couple had an idea. Jesse and Mathilda Beagle had an eight-month-old son named James. He weighed less than 11 pounds. The Beagles decided to mail their son to his grandmother. She lived about a mile away. They bought 15 cents worth of stamps and insured James for 50 dollars. Vernon O. Lytle, a mail carrier, accepted the package

and delivered James safely to his grandmother.

Postage was much cheaper than a train ticket. The weight limit

OHIO

The Baltimore & Ohio Railway mail car in 1913.

6

Number of eggs mailed in one of the first packages sent by parcel post.

- Parcel post service began on January 1, 1913.
- At first, packages could weigh up to 11 pounds.
- In 1914, the weight limit went up to 50 pounds.
- James Beagle was the first baby delivered through the US mail.

for packages increased. By early 1914, parcels could weigh up to 50 pounds. On March 13, four-year-old May Pierstorff was mailed to her grandparents' home in Idaho. She rode in a train's mail car. Her parents attached 53 cents in stamps to her coat. That year, the postmaster general ruled that humans could not be mailed.

Real-Life Event Helps Inspire Whale of a Tale

Early in November 1820, a whale attacked the whaleship *Essex*. A crew member spotted a pod of whales and cried, "There she blows!" The sailors lowered boats into the water. Within minutes, a man harpooned one of the whales. The whale struck back. It hit the boat with its huge tail, putting a hole in it. The crew went back to the *Essex* for repairs.

$556.37
Herman Melville's lifetime earnings from *Moby Dick*.

- In November 1820, a whale attacked the *Essex* and the crew had to abandon ship.
- In a story by a man named Jeremiah N. Reynolds, a whale called Mocha Dick attacked whaling ships.
- Both inspired Herman Melville to write *Moby Dick*.

1834 illustration of the whaleship *Essex* being struck by a whale.

The first mate started fixing the hole. He saw a whale in the distance. The whale moved swiftly toward the ship and rammed his head into it. The force of the blow knocked over the men on board. Swimming faster than before, the whale struck the ship again.

Herman Melville.

THINK ABOUT IT

Have you ever written a story? What inspired you to write it? Where might you get ideas for a story?

The ship began filling with water. The men quickly loaded three boats with food and supplies and climbed in. They were 2,000 miles from South America. Twenty men boarded the boats. Only five would survive the terrible journey back to land.

Author Herman Melville heard about the *Essex*. He read a story by an adventurer named Jeremiah N. Reynolds. The story was called "Mocha Dick: Or the White Whale of the Pacific." Mocha Dick, the story went, won many battles against whaling ships. It crushed boats with its jaws. Broken harpoons were stuck to its back.

The tale of the *Essex* and the story about Mocha Dick inspired Melville to write his own book, *Moby Dick*.

21

Cars Race from New York to Paris—in 1908

Cars lined up for the start of the 1908 race.

22,000
Approximate length in miles (35,405 km) of the New York to Paris car race.

- Two newspapers sponsored the race.
- Six cars started the race, but only three finished.
- It took the winning car 170 days to finish the race.

On the morning of February 12, 1908, an official fired a pistol into the sky over Times Square in New York City. Two hundred fifty thousand spectators cheered. Six cars zoomed away. Three French cars, as well as an American, Italian, and German car, began a long journey. They were to travel the world from New York to Paris. The *New York Times* and the Paris newspaper *Le Matin* sponsored the event.

In 1908, automobiles were just coming on the scene. Many people had never even seen a car. There were no road maps, traffic lights, paved roads, or gas stations.

The race route was very difficult. Drivers traveled across the United States to San Francisco. From there, the American team took a ship to Alaska. The roads through Alaska were impassable. So race organizers changed the course. From Seattle, contestants boarded a ship to Japan. They took another boat to Siberia. Then they crossed Asia and Europe. Only three cars finished the race. They were the American, Italian, and German cars.

The cars crawled through blizzards, sandstorms, mud, and flooded areas. Teams helped each other by digging paths through snowdrifts. Horses pulled cars from swamp-like roads. None of the cars had been built for this kind of ordeal. They had no tops or windshields.

On July 26, 1908, the Germans arrived in Paris. They were first, but they placed second because they had broken some of the race rules. The Americans arrived on July 30 and won first place. It had been 170 days since they left Times Square. The Italians finished third.

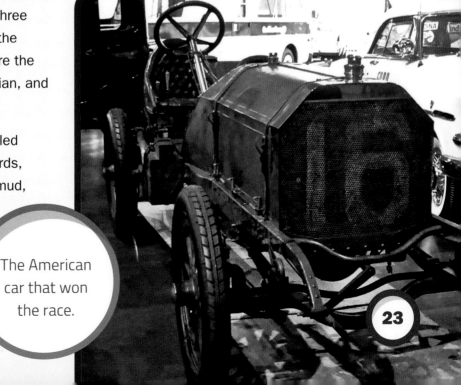

The American car that won the race.

Toxic London Smog Kills Thousands

December 5, 1952, was a cold day in London. People warmed their homes by heaping coal into their furnaces. Chimneys billowed smoke from the burning coal. Power plants and factories spit more pollution into the sky. Soon after, the fog crept in. It swirled together with the smoke, blanketing the city in darkness.

3,000
Gallons of air (11,356 L) an average adult breathes each day.

- The Great Smog of London was created by pollution, fog, and special weather conditions.
- It covered London in darkness and made the air very hard to breathe.
- The Great Smog lasted four days.
- At least 8,000 people died.

Policemen had to use flares to guide traffic on December 8, 1952.

THE CLEAN AIR ACT

Four years after the Great Smog, Parliament passed the Clean Air Act of 1956. The act controlled what people could burn. It required smoke-free areas. It encouraged businesses and homes to move away from coal as a main heating source. But changing to other fuel methods took time. In 1960, another smog covered London. About 750 people died.

Special weather conditions held the smog close to the ground. It was thick and yellow. It smelled like rotten eggs. Black particles covered people from head to toe. They wore masks to protect themselves from the toxic air.

Visibility was near zero. Birds crashed into buildings. People left their cars and walked. Some couldn't see their own feet. Bus service was suspended. Trains and flights were delayed. Sporting events were canceled. The smog even seeped into buildings, causing concerts to be postponed. Crime rose. Robbers broke into stores and houses. They used the smog as a cover.

On December 9, the wind picked up and swept the lethal cloud away. It is estimated that the Great Smog of 1952 killed at least 8,000 people. The elderly, babies, and those with breathing problems were the ones who were affected the most.

Men Are Shanghaied into Being Sailors

Joseph "Bunko" Kelly was a shady character. During the 1800s, he ran boardinghouses for sailors in Portland, Oregon. He would get men drunk or give them drugs. Then he would take them to a ship in the harbor and leave them there. The ship's captain paid Kelly for the men. When the men woke up the next day, the ship was far out at sea. The men were forced to work as sailors for months to come.

Kelly tricked captains, too. It's said that once when he could not find any men in time, he wrapped a wooden statue in canvas and took it to a ship. The captain didn't discover he paid for a statue until it was too late.

Kidnapping men and selling them for sailors was called shanghaiing. Men like Kelly were called crimps. There were many men like Kelly, and a few women. Ships were desperate for sailors. It was a hard job, and once a ship

A drawing of Joseph "Bunko" Kelly from a newspaper in 1893.

reached land, sailors often abandoned ship. Captains were always looking for new workers. Many didn't care where they came from.

Shanghaiing ended for many reasons. Laws were passed that made it harder to crimp. As ships became steam-powered, skilled

$30 to $60

What a captain paid a crimp for a sailor.

- Joseph "Bunko" Kelly was a famous crimp.
- Kelly shanghaied men into working as sailors.
- Shanghaiing was outlawed in 1915.

workers were needed to run them. Not just anyone could be a sailor. Finally, the Seamen's Act of 1915 made crimping a federal crime.

Fact Sheet

Ancient Pompeii, with Mount Vesuvius in the background.

- One of the most famous volcanic eruptions in history happened in Pompeii, Italy, in 79 CE. The volcano, Mount Vesuvius, instantly poured ash all over the city. The thick covering of ash helped to preserve Pompeii. Years later, archaeologists were able to remove some of the ash and study what life in an ancient city was like.

- Orphans weren't the only ones who helped deliver vaccines to sick people. In 1925, a sled dog team raced across ice and snow to get the diphtheria vaccine to Nome, Alaska. Diphtheria is a serious infection that affects the nose and throat.

- The United States Post Office issued the first postage stamp on July 1, 1847. Before then, customers would take their letters to the post office. The postmaster would write the amount of postage due directly on the letter.

- Whaling was a profitable business in the nineteenth century. Whale expeditions sometimes took three to four years. Whale oil was very valuable. It was used for oil lamps and in candles, soaps, and perfumes. Whaling is now illegal in most parts of the world.

- Smog is a serious problem today in many cities around the world. It doesn't kill a lot of people right away, like the Great Smog of London did in 1952. But it has short-term and long-term health effects. Smog can cause coughing and irritate the throat. It can make breathing harder. It can damage the lining of the lungs. Doctors recommend staying indoors when the air quality is poor.

- The first affordable car for most Americans was the Model T. Henry Ford was the developer. He created several assembly-line automobile manufacturing plants. Because of this, cars were built quickly. The price of the Model T dropped from $850 in 1908 to $300 in 1925.

Glossary

boycott
To refuse to buy from a store or company, or go into a place, in order to make a protest or bring about a change.

chasm
A large ditch in the earth.

Communists
Supporters of a political system called communism. With communism, the government owns all property.

debt
A payment that is owed to someone else.

first mate
The person on a ship next in command after the captain.

harpooned
A sharp spear used for hunting whales.

hull
The main body of a boat.

munitions
Weapons used during war.

parcel post
A mail service that hands parcels.

Parliament
In some governments, the group of people who make the laws.

subsidize
To help with the payment of something.

tenants
People who rent properties.

vaccine
A substance that makes people resistant or immune to a disease.

For More Information

Books

Kops, Deborah. *The Great Molasses Flood: Boston 1919*. Watertown, MA: Charlesbridge, 2015.

Macy, Sue. *Motor Girls: How Women Took the Wheel and Drove Boldly*. New York: National Geographic Children's Books, 2017.

Philbrick, Nathaniel. *In the Heart of the Sea: The True Story of the Whaleship Essex*. Young Reader's Edition. New York: Puffin Books, 2015.

Visit 12StoryLibrary.com

Scan the code or use your school's login at **12StoryLibrary.com** for recent updates about this topic and a full digital version of this book. Enjoy free access to:

- Digital ebook
- Breaking news updates
- Live content feeds
- Videos, interactive maps, and graphics
- Additional web resources

Note to educators: Visit 12StoryLibrary.com/register to sign up for free premium website access. Enjoy live content plus a full digital version of every 12-Story Library book you own for every student at your school.

Index

About the Author

Rachel A. Bailey grew up in Kansas. As a child, she loved reading and taking walks with her beloved Australian shepherd. Rachel is a former teacher. She now writes education curriculum and books for children.

READ MORE FROM 12-STORY LIBRARY

Every 12-Story Library Book is available in many fomats. For more information, visit 12StoryLibrary.com

32